Something in the Way
//
Obstruction Blues

Something in the Way // Obstruction Blues

— JOHN DUVERNOY —

Horse Less Press
2014

Something in the Way // Obstruction Blues © John Duvernoy, 2014.
All rights reserved.
First edition printed in the United States.

ISBN: 978-0-9829896-8-5

Front cover image by Gregory Halpern
Back cover image by Ahndraya Parlato
Design & typesetting by HR Hegnauer | www.hrhegnauer.com
Typeset in Perpetua

The publication of this book was made possible through
the generous contributions of our readers and supporters.

HORSE LESS PRESS
www.horselesspress.com

note found pinned to an elm : these poems

*are not from my life none of these things
has ever happened to me   i don't*

live this way

Something in the Way // *Obstruction Blues*

3	//	(sound check)
4	//	As Is
5	//	Where The Cross Roads Used To Be
6	//	The Weather Here
7	//	Rubber Nights
8	//	(for the night's dead weight on gravel ends)
9	//	Grey Are The Woods
10	//	Medium Rare
11	//	The Hysterical Present
12	//	no.3
13	//	Quiet Snow In The Kitchen
14	//	The Hesitant Surface
16	//	After The Cow
18	//	New Mound
19	//	Still Life With Retractable Fire Escape
20	//	(story where the ending is)
21	//	Something In The Way
22	//	Held Head Underwater Until A Name Came
25	//	The Hearse-Men
26	//	Person Hood Blues
27	//	Something About A Knot Eased Loose
28	//	3 Haystacks and a Man
31	//	Personhood Blues
32	//	Wisteria, Magnolia

Something in the Way // Obstruction Blues

51	//	Blue Tarp
53	//	Lake Drag
54	//	(dopamine compost industrial blues)
55	//	Easy, Easy Devil
56	//	(a sandy phone-call)
57	//	December January Cure
58	//	Muleskinner
59	//	The Vicissitudes
60	//	This Film Is Called
62	//	Sorcerer's Flunky
63	//	Shelter From The Mind
64	//	Drone-ism
65	//	The Burials Of Said After Party
66	//	Like So Many Sundowns Before Me
67	//	Death Junket Blues
70	//	June 16th, Vermont
71	//	Aboutness
72	//	Outskirts Earth
73	//	Headturner
74	//	Hair Like Straw
79	//	What The Full Moon Does To The Wolf
85	//	Notes & Acknowledgments
86	//	About The Author

Something in the Way // Obstruction Blues

Hand me my writing blindfold

Now necklace of incipient tongues

AS IS

It was my first six months in Heaven and I hadn't really settled in yet
all day long the lab monkeys mimic our beating off of course the food was
to die for the view out of this world some of it glistened and some of it moved
like glass arrows through rainwater I sipped coffee watched weather same as before
this present eternity perfunctory sniff slit eyes I felt pretty good inside
of my human skull is a pristine rat skull in place of my asshole
an even bigger asshole other than that even here
slithering is both a means and an end.

WHERE THE CROSS ROADS USED TO BE

handsome as the sun
we watched from the

coffinette
while he

sort of eased his hand up
the skirt of the sky and it

came back
articulating

THE WEATHER HERE

I am not going to look at you	I am not going to look at you	This is a strain of my voice
My name is		Because
Of what could happen	If we saw each other	Is why
I'm not going to look at you	(the weather here is what I know of you)	White lightning
Because of what	My eyes will	See in you

RUBBER NIGHTS

I got sent home from work for crying again

which is bullshit cuz I could fly

that plane in my sleep   Pulled up

to the curb in front my father's house and

I couldn't get out

There's nothing worth smoking in here

Drove around the block for a year or two   Glued

a beard and registered to vote for something anywhere

Figured there must be anything somewhere   Pulled books

from shelves for hours desperate for another's line

The insurgents won the pennant   or you made a superstition

out of going alone   Something poutine like that

Rubber nights,
               I put the car in an oasis

(for the night's dead weight on gravel ends)

if you wander away from the picnic, the wolves
but if the picnic is peopled in sheep's clothes
if the wolves are not wolves but far worse, moles

faith is an elastic, an elastic stretched taut when he
was an asphalt, we watched you writhing in the street
try, try to reach the end of this feeling

GREY ARE THE WOODS

Grey are the woods of my true love's childhood dissolve.
Found wanting and not wanting. Found everything in
-ured.

Set back from the dune's edge on a squirt of tar, a swamped
oyster bar. If you thought about it, you couldn't stand -
Her pale hair walking out the door, o tepid packet of mayonnaise.

I watched from a stool the daymoon's miniscule push
and tug on the delicate furniture of throats. Mimed
sucking a lime, mimed knowing you. The drift waved.

Daisy puked ketchup on the shoe of a police horse.
I wouldn't have refused my due while still alive and mugging
of course I am someone else's problem now.

MEDIUM RARE

A thin veil of rain
on the tarmac through
an unmarked door sipping
from a paper cup the sole
of his loafer held on
with a ragged swath of
athletic tape he smells like
the air before an electrical fire
white-haired child staring
out the runway says I never
seen a yellow so red before

THE HYSTERICAL PRESENT

Someone crossed the wires and I received
a surge of happiness.

              I started writing on your
back again, small nouns, saying true things,
behind you.

          Then I flipped my pencil over
and erased the vertebrae.

Rings slip off,

      which is where the strings come in:

(tell me we'll have until
                dawn before they find us

(tell me you'll be wearing
                my breath in your hair

(tell me if ever you
           read this

                And so on.

I moved my lungs in time to it,
                embarrassed for the air.

NO. 3

it was a shale pit put cries of tiny
apples in the air like screwjars
flesh of memory pricking the woods
with a wooden pole what slipped
through an owl came back
a reservoir of tackle   blue
grownups so unknown

QUIET SNOW IN THE KITCHEN

learning to sip
autumn
on the thruway

i could cry on a dime
then it feels like still

redolent of crushed
maple leaves in the
hollow you covet

ratcheting unease
the wind

sustaining
thru my earring

....

swaying knapsack
dark mouth feel

THE HESITANT SURFACE

The sky was a joke
I vowed to remember

To retell it deftly
All winter

It was just what I
Needed underground

At which point
It was too late

So who cares
I had a bad year

It was a night
Of neon splints

And cravenness
One of those flared

Sheering moments
Disguised as a calm

Fractured bath
Room mirror

Confirm to me
It's true: I am

Too good
To be true

....

You can't stay in there forever

AFTER THE COW

Same fear, different poem.
Collapsible home.

Was the poisonade to work this way
from the inside out?

When we found her diary,
our breath fell out.

We sifted the ruins in separate rooms.
After the cow, dark cartoons.

Where the fire chief moonlights as arsonist,
by moonlight, by eggplant.

I locked the door real good with a chair.
Momentum of nowhere, resumed.

Now we'll see
what your mirror
is made of.

Distorted portions
of this bull shit self

Consciousness have appeared
or are forthcoming.

Is what the shards
seem to be saying:

              taut
        lake face

                    over

                teeming
        sea floor

NEW MOUND

Black proboscis extended through the window screen
The air a paste of fresh sweat and banana leaves

I heard the distant sizzle of my tears and thought of Moab
Its rock the color of salmon meat, its earlobes thrumming

STILL LIFE WITH RETRACTABLE FIRE ESCAPE

White haired child says I can see through my eyelids you know to an intervention of
psychic thieves.....caryatids......high green *blips......impossible tenderness of*
the foil slip fitted in a fresh pack of smokes. Inane shit like that.
I noticed he'd lost and found a few more finkish rat teeth.

White says something good needs to happen fast or the whole house walks.
Between the pond and the world, and the juju sky, and the zoophytoid us.
.......de-wish-boned.....tin-hearted....... *fin in our throat..............*I yawned and

said a commonplace thing. Meanwhile, uptown
the firemen bounce in their bunks, recalling old flames.
At least there's still time enough to be beautiful, I lied and lay fat
in the starched municipal grass. I guess I thought the trees
would have done something by now, but they just stand there,

dumb as wood, flat as boards.

Story where the ending is money

Story where the pigment of love

SOMETHING IN THE WAY

lord   troweled   blind   spot
in this land there is no
land   undersong   the teaspoon
clawed   crawl   space

     you

will be there
in some hazel mess

mind tinted body of rain
letting into me

       troutness

HELD HEAD UNDERWATER UNTIL A NAME CAME

Dear friends   Impossible   As a letter   I don't
Dig this   Kind of shit   At all   All that
I remember   Swearing to   Whatever   It takes
Took   Everything   As a letter   Dear friends,

Helicopter   Helicopter   Helicopter   Hive
While I was   Crying   I began to   Cry
The tears   Were as   Tears   In my
Two-dimensional   Self,   Who cares?

Eyeball   Want to be   Held
I want to be   Held and   Yes   Sucked
Out of   Myself   And into   The other
Hovering   Helicopter

Since last   We spoke and   Laughed   Years
Passed   Not   Many   Several
Species   Died   Forever

But really   I was mourning   The opposite   Of loss

Strips   Of dressing   Gauze light   Blue snow

In shadow   Rinsed   His sight   Waking

To this   Now   This new   Elsewhere

Stood steady and   Steadying to   Study the floor   Shoved

A stranger's feet   In his boots   *thinks:*   If I can just

Make it through   That door   Before the   Thinking starts

thinks: But the colors   They are   Are so   Or -

A faint fuzz   Of spring blur   Coats   The trees

And a storm-   Clouded faith   *thinks*   The heart is

A   Stuttering   Fool

Fistfuls of long   Summer grasses   Released

Bright   Bouts of   Weeping, thinking   Of becoming

Apparent, praying   Mantis   In a jam   Jar

From the softly   Pitching   Aluminum   Rowboat

At midnight   We watch   October   Snow

Deliquesce   Into pond   Scum   I am

Still waiting   Out   Your renunciation   Whatever

There is   To drive   Through   Do

The skinning   Of the hills   Alive

Name   Date   Position desired

THE HEARSE-MEN

      We
          are driving
under
          the influence
of the
        killing
floor
        moon

       The
road
     is a
long
      dark
switch

       My
bodyguards
        and I
never
       flinch

PERSON HOOD BLUES

He should have been born two hundred years ago
With his punitive pecker and his bald nutsac

Or so mother consoled him of a day
Predilection for getting mule kicked // Taste of primitive nativity

I remember the water receded so quickly
It left pools of bright plankton writhing in the swales like

Never once even batted
An eye at love still it
Swarmed him unrelentingly

On cigarette butt beach belly up to mosquito sky
Say something special about the trees The trees all grew
Sideways that were planted in his heart

SOMETHING ABOUT A KNOT EASED LOOSE

Curfewed streets, afterallhours, rain-sluiced gutters, and the voice of Lansdowne spiraling. I called this working on my wild, thin mercury novel. I'd been in the spray for an undecipherable period of time. Nothing much good had come of it, no impact on a grand scale. It was like my marriage, which had had its black mountain honeyed moments before sliding inexorably into a lake of mud.

My crepe sole plunged through a soggy phonebook and I felt a stab of memory: *The tender, powdery surface of the bialys dented by your fingertips, which bore odors of sex; also butter, onion, dough, tobacco, newsprint, and coffee.* Menace had a way of intimating its presence on the periphery of a banal flush. This, I now knew, would be neither easy nor good. Nor remunerating much in the way of time or sugar.

Clumps of last autumn had caught in the chain link fence, a tiny rivulet of dawn began trickling through gauze. *We sort of fell in love there for a moment, over tea and apricot despair.*

THREE HAYSTACKS AND A MAN

1

After the delicatessen burned, nothing much happened for awhile
I lay on the trampoline and smoked Luckys

The beauty that buoys this vessel is subliminally corrosive
I fancied myself until the pink cloud turned

2

Fell asleep counting
The sheepish maneuvers
I've edited from the galleys

The fool's gold you
Talked into my head

Makes a sound like fireflies
Trapped in a child's fist

3

Robbed from the sky of early March
In that strange winter when the lost

Geese honked vague threats
Toward our respective bunkers

Where the bitter reserve rye
Was eyed by the hour

They came to live in us
Like black spots on our lungs

Tainting each breath
With a wisp of

Unfiltered truth

PERSONHOOD BLUES

On the bright side I won
the depression contest

There was an accident, I got hit
by a smartcar, it

Probably did me some good

That shit will kill you,
I told myself, regarding memory

The state police came and took you away

I stayed on for a few years as

A clever boy without the brains
to hide the knife   Time

Was my lover and my friend
who stole my lover

If this was a poem,   it could end

wisteria, mag
 nolia

He tugged on his jeans and unzipped the tent
Thrust his head into high summer

Stray clouds like spare lives drifted by
                                        Grew apart

Milkweed spittle on a soft-whiskered chin
Funny feeling something still could happen him

Steel blade churning blue earth

Pair of spotted marlboros

Or a cloud misshapen

                            Cloud

In a shape

They all shy away from

We're in a car   In the woods   Laughing   Dusk cornfield

The blue smoke   Uncurls from our mouths   And hangs around

Just like there's no obstruction   Like we've never even been here before

Then Jonesy falls out laughing   Dark and cheap sunglasses   Says:

For so long I lived so wrong   And strides into the pines   Flip the tape

I found the palest canvas sneakers   Shoved deep beneath the driver's seat

Mark doesn't wear those anymore   He shaved his head

We never really saw him again   In a way   The light drops out suddenly

High beams to pitch dark   If you could see us from above   Just skinny legs

Dangling   Now I've got that queasy curfew feeling all the time

                                                your teeth color of october
                                                here, swallow this

i saw the thrill
trickle down the collarbone

                                                toad on toad

like poetry, after you've gone

same   embedded   tic   to   cry   witch

hazel   came   out   where   mud   was

i   was   raft   of   corrugated   cardboard

voraciously   bereft   while   the   dream   absorbed:

        you   know   i

        can   still

        see   it

        but

        only

        with   the

        whites

        of   my   eyes

Yeah I know him, I knew him
We were good friends then

We were like first cousins, or
A handful of arrowheads

Flung down a well   No,
No I haven't seen him for awhile

                                      Or a horse that would sooner burst
                                      Than quit to carry you

I felt a presence beside me
It was the man with the wooden eye
In his ear There was something I'd

Never smelled before
On his breath Quicksilver
In quicksand A strand

Of recombinant chickenshit
On a tooth that shouldn't be loose
This is how

I came to rub my mind
On the teething field It's all over
Your pants there down by the cuffs-

Hand me my writing blindfold
Now necklace
Of incipient tongues

He used to say life will be
Incomplete or not at all
An orange tractor in a brown field

Isn't it enough to know
They're out there somewhere
Bewildered and clinging to lilacs?

Dazed by the same dark heat But
Why did you make him a mute-
So you'd inherit more searingly

I never should have left that car
Three haystacks and a man
Forever turned Stay

Stay in a constant sweat
Dear stranger you got out
Just in time

prayer flask :

blue moon of the sun keep on declining
                     swallowed advances of evening
    shallow breathing all over you
             shadow sucking up breath

                 : a word that means i saw you
                  in a dream, gazing out from carlos
                  lara vista, wearing a blood-dappled
                  camisole, chewing snails

For one thing
I'm no longer
Clairvoyant

Time's hole
Sucking up
The night

then there was that weird period when we knew we were gonna lose each other and i'd stop by the blue ox to eat cheap cashews with you in the garage you showed me the playboy with madonna in it we dug her armpit hair every once in a while i'd drink a pepsi smoke a camel i guess it was a strange spring everybody already ghosts of themselves

I locked the door and put those old records on

Sent my head
out the window

Up the woods

Saturated
alfalfa field

On a thin
fish string

So much mall incense streaming from stalled family cars

I don't know probably
A high rise somewhere

Or a desert without any sand
He always was bound

To a radiator
Staring a hole through

A depiction of
An eclipse

I can still smell
Where he licked

The spine of my
Sister's yearbook

Like he'd been combing
His hair with barbwire

Anymore than lying dead drunk
On a riverbank

Is finally confronting the sky

    Or a cloud misshapen

            Unspools

  From our throats

              As if summoned

Something in the way

            I can't describe

  Anything anymore

             The blue smoke

  Black parking lot

              Like a cardboard box

  After a night of rain

             Like a tooth

That shouldn't be loose

           Wisteria

       Magnolia

          Molina

Car woods   blue smoke   laughing so
wrong   wrong warped same   same I
almost knew you too   is just what we're
made of   the sieve in the shed   is a
real gone home   Listen :

                          when we go off the road
                          just let it go   let it go

Something in the Way // Obstruction Blues

BLUE TARP

1

I googled myself again last night

Still life with slandered periphery

Awoke in a rumor with no ceiling and no floor

Failure in the image of the father's failure, insubordinate

Penis, a modest success, a small

Town ferocity

2

Pistoned breathing in the blush of dawn.
Shit man,

Just leave me on the lawn and go.
Blue tarp.

Phillips-head heart
In the image of the father's
Stripped heart.

I asked you for awe and you gave me an awl.

Knew it was the same one cuz of the little v-shaped
Notch I'd carved in the sun with my penknife.

The sun beat me up again.
This is my password: The sun

Stood me up. I just lay there, waiting
For the hands to do their thing.

LAKE DRAG

      drug me to the lake
      with the secret pond
      in it take the world
      off my blouse open
      the mouth of the whip
      poorwill's eyes and
                          vie in

(dopamine compost industrial blues)

in a borrowed
station wagon

stabled to my tar
paper heart

that i may walk
the lines of the linoleum

unswerved
we crossed

that dylan song again
and i thought of elizabeth

street you don't know the one in
the passenger seat i bit my tongue

trying to swallow
the whole beyond the sky i know

you're gonna think this
life is just a riff

---

i hadn't held an amulet

in a long time

EASY,
EASY DEVIL

Maniacal need night ushers in, hog
ties you to me, of me, and in, in.
The way the fatback blood is in, deep in,
the stropped and rutted hillside.

A sandy phone-call   A styrofoam cup   Of nescafe   Collar up

Watching the field   Taking my life   That lasted most the night

Cassette of wish   I could forget

All that hums   Whirs   And won't be

DECEMBER JANUARY CURE

The long canoes slip through the cigarette filters like swans going deaf

The fear is beginning to seem like a carving upon the water

Years passed not many in sum a few Sunday drives was all was

Everything startled into still thinking

To shear the mind and tether it to a hissing dream

That, or

                return to our lives fat
                uously unchanged

MULESKINNER

A lot of the gutless things they say

I've done, I've done.

Forgetting you not enough is one.

THE VICISSITUDES

Talking to my Dad about collapsed barns
Not even saying anything really

Just being there
Thinking in

To the same torqued dark door frame
Same wood weathered face

....

I turned my back and
So my back you loved

THIS FILM IS CALLED

Something's happened to my fun
That scared stiff stuffed animal
All roads in this cornfield lead to

It don't rub me the way it did before
Is back in my clothes
Robitussin maize

Smack back in shop class again every time
Chasing a childhood what
A memorable mother

Chasing an adolescence spent
A beautiful buzz saw what
Of pearl handled switchblade

Like a celebrity
I pierced the skin but
There was no within
Other worlds

Passing through a celebrity
(viscera pooling in tin foil shoes)
This film is called
Identical to these

Dozens of shorn and
Harboring a
Dawn
The stump tree

Cupped hands each
Faltering
Was hanging strips of innocence on
Time

Was my lover and my friend
I made a mistake
The years

Who stole my lover
And looked again
Had scarcely touched us

Your hand-
We say
Bloom
Just like that

Writing the way
Bruises
I wish I could stop now
Duck pond

Dark protected cove   To which my heart goes out
And don't return   To swim in the pull of shadow
Beneath her collarbone   To swim there all night
And then to swear off swimming

                               No only

SORCERER'S FLUNKY

The green glass bottle again
My yellow hair   My black
blue hair

                       Live under
this house with us
Where time won't crawl

                         Your spirit
  is uplifting   y

                                     w
               Fl   n   a
                 oa t i
                         g   a

SHELTER FROM THE MIND

After the ecstasy ended, the city refurbished.
Ignoring my nod of the trees.

                       Do the one
where you leave your body, so that your
body may do as it please.

What the others said and thought I knew.
Cantilevers.

        Your brothers are out there

Synesthetic night

                Staking the pith

DRONE-ISM

Took a job in Toledo Ohio
from 1917 to 2003

I impersonated
a person

I looked
over my shoulder

Backing the Pontiac
through the small

Dark corridors

Don't worry darling my ego
gets bigger it's

Just coiled

I winced
for the cameras

In the sky
I watched

From the causeway
while the cause was

Eviscerated

LIKE SO MANY SUNDOWNS BEFORE ME

It makes profound use of its face

I do not know what will become of whatever

Substitute your own noun *in the desert*

of Carlos Lara in the wallpaper of magnolias

and bleeding deer *I think I began to believe in*

spite of myself driving swallowing hovering

whatever etched a smear of its *homily*

in the gravel his passenger eyes

THE BURIALS OF SAID AFTER PARTY

    scythe
          swathed
   through
         moon
     in
         tuberose
   bone
      bent
  spade
      head

(sunrise)

     wept
    at
    and
  spat

DEATH JUNKET BLUES

(study the art of being everywhere/barely there)

the music was covered in fur. the fur was
falling out in tufts. in the exposure where the
tufts had been, bees swarmed. the bees flicked
their honeyed legs across the surface of the music.
sound shivered. the tufts lay in the dust, black as oil.
red ants came on. the sky, once remote, drew in
on the music. puddles parted.

(like the lover's depression in the grass or)

at the edge of the music, a well.
at the bottom of the well, a way.
the way was paved with mistranslation, tape hiss.
sex and or electricity was a wave within the way,
welling up until it drenched the music, blurring every
edge. hence the mistranslation, the reverb.

(a heavy headed father's sleepless dent in a pillow)

the music was wounded, it warbled mucus. the mucus
was contagious, warping sound wherever it smeared.
smear-field, implicating the weave of the modal fabric.
red ants arrove and bent to work unraveling. above the knees
the clouds darkened. in the ditch, the music, its sides heaved.
the many red tongues pushed in and out. a practiced imitation
of listening.

JUNE 16TH, VERMONT

This is not a letter to beg you remember your favor for me. I'm in a darkened lecture hall watching an early Ingmar Bergman show. But it looks like a thousand meditations of gray. And maybe I wish this could be the kind of letter I said before. If vacillating words could do such things, which you and I both know they can, but not ours, not here.

The woman to my left, one row in front of me, keeps raising a green glass bottle, pouring it calmly down her throat. I keep my eyes on the screen, the shirts and shoes of light, listen to her swallow. If coruscating words could do such things, which you and I both know they can.

Feel what leads means to you in the sentence one thing leads to another. The film is good, the modulations. I'm reading none of the dialogue and the woman has emptied her beer. The green glass bottle alone on the arm rest. I feel a tenderness toward it like no other.

ABOUTNESS

Now I'm permanently chilled and sweating both

Like sun dried tomatoes steaming in a jar of milk

This isn't going very well is it?

Through the small dark corridors

Though I have my vagrant loyalties

I know someone who knows someone, etcetera

It's all very hush-hush

Like a celebrity passing through

A celebrity

You know my poetry it keeps

Me alive but it

Don't exist

OUTSKIRTS EARTH

Winter sun's tongue traced the spit-shined
anus under the sky.

       The knee-high snowflowers
began to lasso their roots at the butcher's
sleigh.

In the piney woods, a cleaving place
spirits the moon inside a cake dish,
shortest day.

We congregate in the spill. Thought we can feel
streaming instants underneath.

Blue clot of light slides over the iris.
Mineral tang.

(any day now, passing through, dear life, the dear dead
(life will arrive, any day now and in passing, i'll drop every name i know

HEADTURNER

I wasn't following her, or if I was I didn't know it. A bleached blonde

Mirage. A tincture of teardrop tobacco and lavender soap. Nothing

Has changed save my point of view. The sky, a delicate plume

Of puce dried blunt and black. Now I'm you.

The moon, and its pulsating blood clot.

She had a way of irradiating everything in her path.

Small brown birds dropped dead in the street.

I snatched one beneath my poncho while coolly appraising the mannequin's figure.

It was alright, but inert, and suddenly I felt like a dullard's idea of a creep.

There was supposed to be another shark attack.

That's why I came here.

That, and to get the hell away from wherever I was.

This   deserted   taffeta   beach
                                        The   sun
Behind   a   tuft   of   spun   sugar

HAIR LIKE STRAW

1

Story where the
incremental soul
plateaus

Spittoons

2

For if I am living on the verge of a knowing that never
Like a room with a view of a room with no door
For if I am not on my way to you

3

There, I said it.

I bit off the prick of the contortionist
when he bent over backwards for you,

>   in you.
>   I kept

sniveling watch at your desk while
our life was deloused and spayed.

4

Story where time macerates

....

Your name in his mouth

5

Hair like straw, straw wine
in a tin field.

Hauling out skeins of blood melon
and gold rind.
           The sky in
flattened pieces on the pond.

Beneath a penny moon, memorizing
rooms through blown curtains, driving

driving by.
The failure

                    of literature
                    cools my face.

WHAT THE FULL MOON DOES TO THE WOLF

•

I watched the earth swallow my bones whole, and I felt lighter, less attached.
  (my eyes were in the eaves)   Empiricism, he said, the hooves careen.
Will-o-the-wisp, you turn the river around. (fallen sun, creosote flare)

•

From the tinted window of a slow-moving car, your perfume traces.
Which meaning did you have in mind (revelator)? Of the vaporous night air
you breathe in, I am even jealous.

•

It's like we met at the mouth of a cave and tunneled in.
Past the brown bat, the black bear, the silverfish light of our useless
appendix shining.

•

Now we've arrived where? The air is historical, meretricious. Is it us
or the earth that keeps going in deniable, irreversible circles.
Must we contend with the echo of all we have ever uttered

      in the undressed dark of one another

•

You are marrying the wrong manifesto.   Strawberries and cream
grow on trees.   (fall on me)

•

(when your breath starts to spit in quick thimbles and the curtain sucks into
 the window's mouth, your body quakes to say itself, seeing minnows)

•

I swallowed the river to watch the fish flail, I failed you.
You were always blinking, missing my good moments, a car door
slamming in the night.

•

(remember when the words that almost left your
 ruby lips stirred the jewels in my yellow hair)

•

The letter should have reached you by now

Had I written it

•

Somewhere in this city you are   I would say this to you   Or if not this
city then one exactly like it: Trade wallets with me

To let the rabbi dab at this pain   If it's snowing I'm your fiancé
Then I went away and then   I went away,

               in my place was a blur

•

What the full moon does to the wolf

•

If only I could sleep in your coat   (revelator)

It is a detriment to my character, this fondness for looking
up your skirt, down your shirt, between the lines of what no one ever says

Bringing you flowers from *substitute your own noun*'s grave

.

I came to in a white mustard field, eye shadow in the trees.

.

A russet apple   the furred earth   the blue shale   will you
If all the ewoks have been poached from your california

clear out of this world

.

Queer angle of the winter sun, concussion concession smell.
You stood in the bleachers and watched the zamboni erase all trace of us.
Eye of slush, mind of slush, flat-headed diamondshovel.
I will hold this against you until it melts.

.

(i can smell the candy bar on your breath
 thin green light of the radio dial
 reflecting off your eyeteeth we are
 driving all night through the)

.

For all I know your heart didn't break, the details are just pixels to us now.
The thing is to ignore yourself all the way,   as a circle.
Since nothing is itself,   we won.

·

I love what you've done with the spaces my life used to fill.

  (speckled newts blooming from the rent mound)

My only regret is a beautiful and endless killing song.

·

NOTES & ACKNOWLEDGMENTS

Some of the poems in this book repurpose phrases and fragments of language originally sung by the following artists: Sarah Riggs, Charles Thompson, Leonard Michaels, Forrest Gander, Jenny Boully, Rene Crevel, Tom Waits, Cormac McCarthy, Anne Carson, Denis Johnson, Michael Burkard, Bob Dylan, John Ashbery, CD Wright, Don Delillo, Roberto Bolano, Mary Ruefle, Jason Molina, Barry Hannah.

I would like to thank the following editors for their support in publishing earlier versions of some of the poems in this book: Christopher Lura (*Paul Revere's Horse*), Micaela Morrisette (*Conjunctions*), Mia Lipman (*Canteen*), Jen Tynes, Jennifer Denrow, Erika Howsare & Michael Sikkema (*Horse Less Review*), Kate Wolf (*Night Papers*), Timothy Liu & Timothy Donnelly (*Boston Review*), Thibault Raoult (*Realpoetik*), Albert Abonado (*The Bakery*), Zachary Schomburg & Mathias Svalina (*Octopus*), Michael Bernstein & Michael Crake (*Pinstripe Fedora*), Wendy Duren & Katie Perkins (*Bennington Review*). Thanks, as well, to the following organizations for crucial support during the writing of this book: The Vermont Studio Center, The Millay Colony for the Arts, The Boomerang Fund for Artists.

A special thanks to the Horse Less Crew (Jen Tynes, Michael Sikkema, Erika Howsare, Jennifer Denrow) for their tireless dedication and integrity. Thank you to Ahndraya Parlato and Gregory Halpern for the generous use of their photographs, and to HR Hegnauer for the sterling design.

Love without end to my extraordinary family and brave friends - **thank you**.

this book is for Jonna, who keeps my inkwell full

ABOUT THE AUTHOR

John Duvernoy was raised in the hills of Central New York, with his three brothers. He now lives with his wife in the Pacific Northwest.